alfie's POetic Tales

M C Davies

authorHOUSE®

AuthorHouse™ UK
1663 Liberty Drive
Bloomington, IN 47403 USA
www.authorhouse.co.uk
Phone: UK TFN: 0800 0148641 (Toll Free inside the UK)
*   UK Local: 02036 956322 (+44 20 3695 6322 from outside the UK)*

Published by AuthorHouse 07/29/2021

ISBN: 978-1-6655-9132-4 (sc)
ISBN: 978-1-6655-9131-7 (e)

Library of Congress Control Number: 2021914433

Print information available on the last page.

Contents

◇◇◇◇◇◇◇◇◇◇

Alfie Moon the Little Poochow

❖❖❖❖❖❖❖❖

He's my little babaloo
He will fit inside my shoe
He is curly black and white
He is friendly he do not bite
He also lives in my cocoon
And his name is Alfie moon
Alfie likes to play all day
He's cute and funny in a comical way
He likes a little fuss and a cuddle to
He also likes chicken believe me he do
When he's tired he'll sit on my lap
And go to sleep like a good little chap

My Little Lifeguard

Barney go and get your lead, there's a good lad
I'm taking you for a walk said John my dad
We are going to the beach where you can run so free
Barney! Go and fetch the stick, I've thrown it in the sea
Then we walked along the beach playing with a ball
I brought it back again when I heard a loud call
A boy was in difficulty, so I swam out to him
He held onto my collar with one little limb
Oh God bless you said his mother you've saved my little boy
You're the bravest little dog I've just got to buy you a toy
I'm so proud of you Barney I don't know what to say
Wait till we get home we'll tell mam about your day

kat the Cat and alfie the Dog

Good morning Kat said mam, where have you been
I've been hunting mice, but there's not one to be seen
I'm tired now and want to sleep in my chair
That's my chair Alfie, your settee is over there
He opened one eye and said go away I'm tired
If you don't get off, your face won't be admired
Kat jumped up on the chair biting Alfie on the nose
He yelped so loud falling down on his toes
Alfie ran to mam to show what Kat had done
She put a plaster on his nose now that's better son
It's time to make up as you've got your own place
Yes they said licking one another's face
Mam sat in her chair saying well fancy that
They've cuddled up together sleeping on the fluffy mat

The Mischievous Pair

◇◇◇◇◇◇◇◇◇◇

Be good Lola and Alfie said mam going out through the door
Yippee said Lola to Alfie as they ran across the floor
Let's call our friends in to come and play with us
We were told to behave said Alfie, oh stop making such a fuss
She opened the flap and called out to the squirrel and rabbit
I'm telling you Lola you must not make this a bad habit
They ran around playing with the toys and a ball
Knocking over a vase and down it would fall
A car pulled up then heard a key in the door
They scurried to the flap as Lola said go quick go
Mam called out to the dogs, what is all this mess here
I don't know said Lola, as Alfie went to say her
So Lola jumped and bit Alfie on the cheek
Serve you right said Lola as he was going to let it leak
Get into your baskets and stay there for the night
And do not move until the morning breaks light
The grandchildren smiled thinking this is not new
As I think they know something about them don't you?

My Little Pal

I am a little pony my name is Palforme
I live on the farm with all my friends especially a boy named Sammy
He rides on my back nearly every day because he cannot walk
His parents keep an eye on him and watches like a hawk
Then one day a fire started in the little barn
They all shouted Sammy Sammy, so in the barn I ran
I caught his jumper and dragged him out away from all the fire
Well done little pony you've saved his life
we look up to you and admire
Sammy cried out where's my pony my little Palforme
I love you little pony you are my best friend you are my pal for me

The Cockerel and the Fox

Rooster the cockerel sat on his perch and sang cock-y-doodle-doo
He woke all the animals on the farm and the farmers to
Mr. Farmer went around all the animals to make sure they've been fed
We waited for Mrs. Farmer who feeds us
with corn and plenty of bread
The hens were let out for today to play in the summer sun
All day long they had some fun knowing they were safe in the run
Along came a fox, "Please help me Mr. Rooster
I'm sorry for the things I have done"
Hide in the coup you'll be safe in there as
they heard a bang from a gun
When danger passed Mr. Rooster said
"Don't forget your promise to us
We'll leave you some milk and corn every
day we won't tell or make a fuss
Then one day the fox brought his mate and his little youngster
Mr. Rooster he said come and meet my mate
and my cub called little Rooster
He's named after you as you saved my life
and you'll always be my friend
We'll never let anything happen to you as
we'll always be here to defend

How Daisy Became Famous

Daisy why aren't you allowed to go into the milking shed
I have very little milk so I won't get extra to be fed
There's plenty of corn in the field over there
So Daisy ate the corn until a little patch was bare
The farmer phoned the vet to come out to the farm
Please look at Daisy when you've finished with the lamb
Daisy's fine he said only her milk is so thin
It's no good said the farmer yes it is said the
daughter it's good for dieting
Yippy said his youngest daughter we can have
corn flakes and skimmed milk for tea
Well Daisy you're the only cow in the world who
produces skimmed milk for us free

The Unusual Couple

My name is Doug and I am a big slug
I live in the garden feeling very smug
As a beautiful butterfly just landed by me
I feel quivery and shaky as you can see
Hello Miss Butterfly are you enjoying the sun
"Yes" she said "my name is Amber and I'm having such fun"
You are welcome to join me on my cabbage plant
I will understand if you say you can't
I'd be much obliged she said as they sat to have lunch
As they both shared a cabbage leaf and away they did munch
Will you come and see me said the big black slug
"Of course I will," said Amber as she gave a little hug
We'll invite our friends and have a cabbage patch ball
And we'll have a great time every one and all
I've got to go now as it's getting so late
I will come very soon as you're my new friend and best mate

Harry the Hamster

I'm Harry the hamster who lives in a cage
I belong to Tommy who's nine years of age
He gives me plenty of food and water every day
There is also a big wheel for me to play
One day I got out and our cat frightened me
So I ran into a hole thinking it was safe you see
Don't cry little hamster you'll be alright in here
Said a little mouse be very quiet and don't stir
Then the cat will go away believing no ones in
And then he'll stop scratching and that's how we'll win
Harry Harry called Tommy crying out for him
I'm here said Harry running to him in a whim
I was put in my cage then a few nights passed by
When little mouse came to see me he's such a good guy
He came into my cage just to play with me
We'll be best friends for ever and ever wont we

Mr. Oakley the tree

◇◇◇◇◇◇◇◇◇◇

I am a little Oak tree who's living on my own
In the middle of a big field feeling all alone
My branches are drooping because I'm very sad
I've no one to talk to I'm wondering am I bad
Then one day a little black bird landed down on me
He started to build a nest and was busy as a bee
Hello Mr. Blackbird are you coming here to stay
Yes if we can as my mate is coming today
She'll be staying in our nest till the little ones are born
Oh I am so glad said Mr. Oakley I'll listen for her until dawn
Then a squirrel came running going around and around my trunk
Please Mr. Oak tree can I have some acorns to put in my bunk
"Of course you can," said Mr. Oakley but please don't make a sound
As there's blackbirds in their nest and there's plenty on the ground
Mr. Oakley was very happy and his branches spread out in the sun
He stood so tall his leaves were green and didn't mind being only one

a Good Deed

Don't cry little girl please don't cry
I would like to help you, I don't mean to pry
Who is that the little girl cried, it's me the Oak tree
I'm called Mr. Oakley I'd like to help you, you see
I've lost my necklace and I've looked every where
My mam and dad bought it from the town over there
It was bought for my birthday, I only had it for a week
Mr. Oakley my name is Rachael please help me to seek
Don't worry little Rachael I will call Mr. Blackbird
Send for the magpies and tell them they must give me their word
When they find the necklace they must bring it back to me
Instead of stealing all that glitters, they'll do a good deed you'll see
Then the magpies were looking all over the
field until one shouted out I found it
They handed the necklace to Mr. Oakley
and said now we have done our bit
Thank you, oh thank you said Rachael you
will always be my best friend
Especially Mr. Oakley whom we all love, trust and always depend

 # Speedy the tortoise

Tarquin the tortoise is very sad and walking along so slow
Alfie said "what's the matter Tarquin why are you so low
I'd like to play but I can't keep up with you
and your friends in the park
I have a great idea said Alfie come inside the shed giving a little bark
There's two pairs of skates so try them on and see if they will fit
"Yes," he said as he whizzed around then keep them with this kit
Oh thank you Alfie can we go to the park to play a game of football
"Yes," said Alfie as they played half way
through and nobody scored at all
Then Tarquin whispered to Alfie kick it as
high and long as you can get
To their surprise he darted under their legs
and headed the ball in the net
Hoorah Alfie's side shouted we have won the
game as they patted the Tortoises shell
They picked him up and tossed him about
then he knew that all will be well

The Seaside Donkey's

Come on little donkeys the seasons starting
we've got to go to the beach
One by one the six of us followed our master
as we stuck to him like a leech
Once on the sands the children came running
shouting please can we have a ride
So the donkeys took the children down the
shore and back again with the guide
What's the matter little boy said Davy the donkey I
want a ride but my mother said I'm to small
You can have a ride on Yorrie as he's gentle as
a lamb and he will not let you fall
Dinner time came we were fed and watered
before the afternoon started again
A little girl lost her money in the sand and
was looking everywhere in vein
We will let you ride Yorrie said Davy as
the others are a little bit too fast
The evening came we were all very tired
and glad when the day had past

Why am I always at the end said Yorrie is it because I'm slow
Well said our master D is for Davy O for Ollie N for Nelly K for
Kelly and Y for Yorrie spells donkey that's why you're last in the row
We were put in our stables where we fell fast asleep
and didn't stir all through the night
It was a donkey that gave Mary the mother of
Jesus a ride as it says in the bible its right

The adolescent ferrets

Bernie and Ernie are two little ferrets who always get into trouble

The two little brothers looks so much alike their

mistaken for one another's double

They play in the garden chasing each other

knocking things down everywhere

You have broken most of the ornaments around

the garden and not it is nearly all bare

Behave yourselves said their mother its time

you knew right from wrong

Your teenagers now it's time to grow up as

this has gone on for too long

You blame one another because we can't

tell and don't care one little bit

We will get you collars with your names written

on them and make sure that they will fit

Don't go running on the lawn, so behave yourselves said our mother

Pretending to listen knowing it will only go in

one ear and out through the other

As she was pulling out the hose and fixing the sprinkler to the tap

This will teach you to behave showering over

their heads hoping they will stop

They loved the water it's the best thing mum could have done

Running under the water darting in and
out they were having lots of fun
Oh well said mum that was a waste of time
now they'll have to learn the hard way
It's time to come in their mother said as
you know it's the end of the day

Mending his ways

Phyllis is a beautiful goose she had an admirer named Sid
Sid is also a handsome goose but Phyllis don't like anything he did
She hissed at him and told him he had better alter his ways
Bending his head he went away thinking about this for a few days
In a few days he went back to her asking her where have I gone wrong
I know I'm good looking and I am in good
health and I'm also very strong
It's not your looks it's the way you treat the
others and now there's only a few
You hiss at them all the time we'll never have any friends with you
So he started being friendly they all looked up to him with surprise
I'm sorry for being horrid I'd like to make
amends and maybe it's time I was wise
Sid then found out it was better to be nice
and Phyllis could see he was trying
Then Sid and Phyllis got together putting his
wings around her and started sighing
Every time they went out Sid was so friendly
that Phyllis thought he was going dafter
They were walking down the lane holding wing
to wing and lived happily ever after

Honey

I am a little busy bee I work all summer time long
I belong to a big huge family together we are strong
I go from flower to flower picking up pollen on the way
I deliver it to the beehive and that is where I stay
I met a little woodpecker tapping on a tree
Hello Mr. Woodpecker I'm Honey I'm a busy little bee
Some of my family are busy making honey for the pots
It's good for healing when you're hurt especially for little tots
I know I've got a terrible sting it's only when I'm tense
It's when I'm being threatened I'll use it for defence
So long Mr. Woodpecker I hope I'll see you soon
I've got to take this pollen to the beehive this afternoon

a Tail to Remember

Oh little piggy wont your tail curl anymore
No said piggy I caught it in the barn door
They took me to the vet to see what he could do
He bandaged it and said you have broken it in two
All the animals laughed at me it makes me very sad
Don't take any notice of them they are just being bad
That pipe over there I'll shape it with my tool kit
I'll wrap your tail around it hoping it will fit
We'll leave it on for a week and a day
Let's hope by then it will curl and stay
My mam looked on saying what a good idea
When time came to take it off I cried a little tear
I was praying so hard and afraid it would fail
Hooray they shouted the curl is back and the spring is in my tail
Thank you oh thank you as I jumped for joy
I am so glad I thought of it said the farmer's boy
I walked passed the animals my head held high
You can't make fun of me anymore (Pointing
to his tail) because that's why

The Park

◇◇◇◇◇◇◇◇◇◇◇

In the park I'd like to run
Come and join me we'll have some fun
Molly and Chee Chee, and Charlie to
And all our other friends come please do
The rabbits are hiding so timid and shy
Play with us bunnies we'd love you to try
The squirrels are hiding high up in the tree
The birds in the sky flying so free
We are gods little creatures for you to know
Maesteg Park is the best place to go
Time is passing I've got to go soon
Please don't forget us I love you
From little Alfie Moon

a Tale of Two friends

◇◇◇◇◇◇◇◇◇◇

As I was walking through the park
In the distance I heard a bark
I ran down the lane and round the bends
And there they were my two little friends
Jim and Wyn I woofed out in vein
I've come to play with you again
Hooray woof woof we'd love to play
We'll have some fun we'd love to stay
Time passed by we'll see you soon
Till next time Jim and Wyn said, To Alfie Moon

Charlie Brown

I am a Jack Russell, My name is Charlie Brown
I chew lots of things and get everyone down
I jump on the settee and land on the cat
She swipes me with her paw and said fancy that
So mam and dad said go and get your lead
We'll take you for a walk over the field
At the corner of my eye I could see Mr. Rabbit
He knows I'll chase him as it's such a bad habit
I ran so fast falling down by a hole
Who's looking straight at me was Mr. Mole
My master called out you're coming with us
I don't know what they're on about or what's all the fuss
I'm only a Jack Russell who likes to play
I try to be good nearly everyday

My Marybell

There is a little lamb who's had a bad fall
She fell through the railings and bounced like a ball
I got to the road and thought she was dead
But was standing right there shaking her head
She was frightened and scared calling out for her mam
And the mother was calling for her little lamb
I wrapped a coat around her and took her home
Look after your baby make sure she doesn't roam
So they stayed by my gate all the year round
Day or night that's where they'll be found
This is a true story we'd like to tell
That's how I named her my Mary Bell

Bell on the farm

◇◇◇◇◇◇◇◇◇◇

My friend Mary bell is a sweet little lamb
She lives by the mountain on Tonnu Road farm
Mary bell I asked are you coming to play
I will but my ma said I'm not allowed to stray
For there's foxes out there who'll come after me
Don't be daft Mary bell I'll look after you said little Alfie
Come we'll play with our friends and have some fun
We'll hop skip and jump till the day is done
Go home Mary bell you'll have to go now
As it's bedtime for all said little moo cow
I've got to go too said little Alfie Moon
We can meet here tomorrow by the afternoon
May god bless the animals that's all around
Goodnight and sleep tight and don't make a sound
SH SH SH ZZZZZZZZZZZZZ.

Lost and found

Little kitten, little kitten where have you been
I'm lost and my mother and she's nowhere to be seen
You can come home to us said Cougar the cat
And lie by the fire and sleep on the mat
There's a saucer of milk and a bite to eat
If you want to be strong then down all that meat
What is your name they wanted to know
Its Dusty he said and it's time I should go
No No said Shadow you'll get lost out there
We'll look after you and they all agreed yeah
Six weeks he stayed in before he could roam
I'm so happy to be here I'm glad it's my home
I play with my toys and my little ball
And jump on the settee and down I'd fall
I curl up in my basket so cosy and warm
They've all adopted me keeping me safe from harm.

Our Secret Adventure

Missy and Kizzy went into the woods
To see their friends whom they understood
Hello Mr. Owl who's high up in the tree
He opened one eye please don't disturb me
O.K they said and went on their way
Good morning Mrs. Mouse will you play today
I can't I'm busy I have little ones at home
I've got to make sure that they don't roam
Good luck Mrs. Mouse we'll see you again
We'd better get back before it will rain
On the way home all the squirrels were playing
At the top of the tree that's where they were staying
Hello Mr. and Mrs. Squirrel your family's having fun
I wish we could join you but our day is done
We're on our way home before it gets dark
Passing little puppies we could hear them bark
We've had a good day their all looking well
It's our little secret SH SH SH we must not tell

Marley's New Year

The music's playing the Highland fling
I twirled and danced doing my thing
Marley's my name I'm a Scotty dog
They dressed me up like a Christmas log
I have lots of toys that is under the tree
I ran to get them then the tree fell on me
I licked from the glasses that was on the floor
Oh dear I felt funny and strangely so poor
There was plenty of food and chews to eat
I could not look at it I just crawled to my feet
I crawled around my head felt so light
So I laid in my basket for the night
The musicians were playing Auld Lang Syne
Everyone's dancing all straight in a line
Happy New Year I barked out with joy
Go to sleep little Marley and be a good boy

My best friend Poppy

Poppy I called are you coming to play
I'll ask my mother and see what she'll say
You can play in the garden she said for a while
As the grass has been cut and put in a pile
We played with a ball and sniffed all around
Look Poppy there's our other friends on the ground
The spiders, the beetles, granny greys and the ants
Don't lay down or they'll crawl in your pants
Watch where your treading and don't step astray
Or they won't come and join in for us to play
Poppy and Molly it's time to come in
Go and eat your food or it'll land in the bin
It's time to go home Molly and Poppy to bed
I was feeling sleepy as I lay down my head
Mum blew me a kiss I could feel a little breeze
She whispered I love you my little Bichon fries

at the Dog Show

Trotter I called will you come back to me
Get your nose from there you'll get stung by a bee
Listen to your mother she's the best to teach you
You'll never be ready when the trials are due
He's the funniest and scruffiest lurcher dog
He ignores a stick carries on with a jog
Come stand in line and receive a rosette
He had it for being the funniest yet
When he got home it was put on the wall
And looks in the mirror feeling ten feet tall
Oh said Rodney wait till I'm bigger
I'll bring one twice the size with a little snigger
Blue the mother said stop this at once
Just get into bed and don't you dare pounce
So go to sleep and be very good boys
In the morning you can play with all your toys

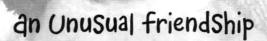

an Unusual friendship

◇◇◇◇◇◇◇◇◇◇

Hello Miss Judy are you coming to play
I'm with my master and I've got to stay
So the golden lab went round the park
I ran across the field and gave a bark
Alfie called Miss Judy as she's passing by
Come and walk with me keep up and try
I will said Alfie though I'm small in size
You can teach me a lot as I know you are wise
We look funny together as I'm little and you're tall
We couldn't care less unless our mothers would call
Can we both walk together next time we meet
Of course you can Alfie looking down by her feet
It's time to go home we can meet here soon
So long Miss Judy you're brilliant from little Alfie Moon

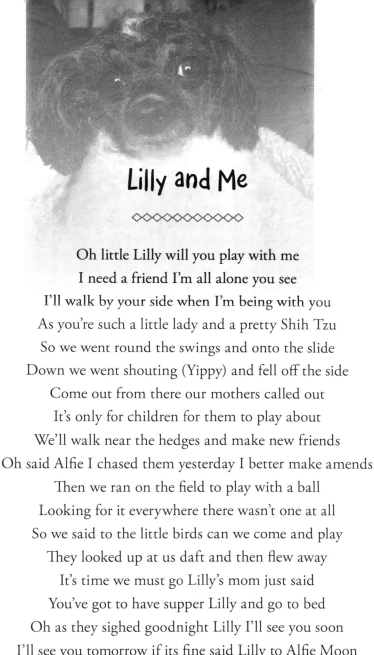

Lilly and Me

◇◇◇◇◇◇◇◇◇◇

Oh little Lilly will you play with me
I need a friend I'm all alone you see
I'll walk by your side when I'm being with you
As you're such a little lady and a pretty Shih Tzu
So we went round the swings and onto the slide
Down we went shouting (Yippy) and fell off the side
Come out from there our mothers called out
It's only for children for them to play about
We'll walk near the hedges and make new friends
Oh said Alfie I chased them yesterday I better make amends
Then we ran on the field to play with a ball
Looking for it everywhere there wasn't one at all
So we said to the little birds can we come and play
They looked up at us daft and then flew away
It's time we must go Lilly's mom just said
You've got to have supper Lilly and go to bed
Oh as they sighed goodnight Lilly I'll see you soon
I'll see you tomorrow if its fine said Lilly to Alfie Moon
So home they all went and slept all night
And did not wake until the morning light

Billy the farm hand

Billy the goat who looks after the field
He's busy eating apples as long as their peeled
The horses are neighing saying Billy look up
There's a dog in the field with her little pup
Hello Billy goat can I stay here today
To show you my pup and to see what you'll say
I'd like to teach him not to chase sheep
Will you help me before you go to sleep
Yes said Billy the goat what shall I do
Pretend to be one of them and chase him to
Watching over there is a calf and the cow
Also a sty full of piglets and a sow
They are all looking at us running back and fore
We are all worn out it is time we must go
So long Mr. Billy goat and all your friends
I'll try and come tomorrow as it all depends
If not tomorrow I'll come when I can
By the way Billy his name is tyke and I'm Nan.

Ratty the Rat

There's a rat over there quick get up on a chair
I'd like to make friends he said I wish you would care
Why you don't like me I don't know at all
My name is Ratty rat and I'm only small
We'll be your friends said Bodie and Skip
And play in the garden till we need a kip
So they ran around and played hide and seek
Time passed so quickly he stayed for a week
Tom cat came along now there's a fat rat
Bodie and Skip shouted hide there's a cat
So he ran in a hole that went down in the ground
Afraid to move and didn't make a sound
They called down to ratty and said it's all clear
I must go home now with a look of fear
When its safe come again said the dogs
I will my friends as I disappeared through the logs
The dogs said to one another he's a great little chap
Let's go inside now we could do with a nap

The Life of a Mouse

At the bottom of the garden there's a tiny house
Sleeping inside is a little mouse
He gave a yawn jumping up oh it's late
I've got to go as I'm meeting my mate
Off he went meeting her by the shed
They loved one another so they got wed
Running through the grass and having fun
Playing for hours till the day is done
So they went to the tiny house for the night
Cuddled up together till it was light
Said Mrs. Mouse we've got to get food
Yes he said quickly changing his mood
The big Tom cat is coming from next door
We'll lie down here in the corner of the floor
When it is safe we'll get something to eat
Over the field there is plenty of wheat
He said we should go back to our little house
I love you she said I love you to Mrs. Mouse
We smiled so much we burst into laughter
And so the story goes we lived happily ever after

The Street

Mrs. Mouse cried Mrs. Hedgehog I have nowhere to go
I've two small babies and I can't look anymore
Well build you a house in the garden next to ours
It won't take us long just a few hours
We can build some more and call it a street
Our friends can paint and make them all neat
When their finished we'll have a street party
Everybody will come even Mr. Mouse called Marty
As the queen is having her birthday soon
We can hang our bunting and flags from our room
When the day came everybody had fun
Plenty to eat and games to be won
Mrs. Mouse said Mrs. Hedgehog you are a good friend
If you ever need or want me I'll always attend
I've got to go now to put my babies to bed
They are feeling sleepy and want to lay down their head
Goodnight Mr. and Mrs. Mouse as I gave them a nod
You'll always be in my thoughts as I pray to God.

Pippa and me

◇◇◇◇◇◇◇◇◇◇

How are you little Alfie said Pippa today
Shall we run around the field and we can play
I can run after you and you could chase me
So try and keep up said little Alfie
Join us little rabbits no hopping just run
And squirrels playing joining in the fun
The children weren't here they were back in school
We all ran to the water and dipped in the pool
When they came out Pippa said I'm feeling cold
We'll go and run around said Alfie being bold
Our masters are calling said Alfie to Pippa
Can I play with you said a Scottie called Skipper
You can come tomorrow as we've got to go now
We can't stay no longer or we'll get a row
So we'll all meet here by this little rock
Be here on time around eleven o'clock

Wiggly the Worm

I'm wiggly the worm living under the ground
The way to the surface is where I'll be bound
I poked my head out it was shining so bright
So I put on my sunglasses to protect my sight
I've got to look out that the birds don't see me
Or they'll have me for dinner as I'm tasty you see
Well well Miss Wiggly it's so good you are out
Said Kusha and Tess we'll give you a shout
If there's any danger we'll chase them away
Go and enjoy yourself for the rest of the day
Miss Wiggly went looking for a tasty leaf
Let me tell you dogs it's as good as your beef
I've got to go now as my family will wonder
I went near my home then I wriggled down under

The Love of a Ball

George and Louis are you coming to the park
Yes we are as they answered with a bark
Go get your ball the yellow and the blue
They can tell the difference believe me it's true
Then their master took them to the park to play
As they are always on time nearly everyday
Good morning Alfie come and play with us
I can't catch a ball but I know how to focus
We'll run with you Alfie for a little while
But as you can see it's just not our style
We are going to play with the ball again
As it won't be long before it will rain
We'll meet here tomorrow for you to know
This is the best park for us dogs to go
So long George and Louis I'll see you soon
Thanks for being my friend said little Alfie Moon

Mrs. Hedgehog and Mr. Mole

Oh Mrs. Hedgehog please don't cross the road
You're not like the children who've learnt the Highway Code
I've got to get to the other side to go into the field
As I've left my babies unattended and no one's there to shield
Don't cross by here said Mr. Mole as it's quite a nasty bend
I'm very grateful to you and you'll always be my friend
They crossed the road ran into the field and there her babies were
Quick said Mr. Mole go and hide as I can hear a purr
It's the big black cat belonging to the farm
he's always roaming around
I've got to go quick said Mr. Mole as I've got to be homeward bound
My family is safe thanks to you Mr. Mole
and I'll keep them from all harm
Please come and see us very soon as we'll always be here on the farm

The Otter family

Mr. Otter is living where no one knows
Right in the country where the river flows
He jumps in the water and loves to swim
No one can see him as it's quite dark and dim
He dives under the water and catches some fish
And takes them home as it's a tasty dish
Mrs. Otter he said there's some fish for tea
Feed the little one's first before you give me
If it's not enough I'll go out and get more
There's plenty for all there's no need to go
After tea they went down to play by the river
It's cold the little ones cried as they gave a little shiver
You'll soon get warm as you play and have fun
Time passed so quickly it's late we must run
When they got home they snuggled into bed
Goodnight mam and dad as they lay down their head
Mam and dad answered goodnight and sleep tight
So we cuddled all together until it was light

The Little Robin

Little Robin red breast flew down to the ground
He was pecking here and pecking there and looking all around
He found a worm and ate it and feeling very full
He found some lining for his nest it was lamb's wool
It's snowing and a blowing and very very cold
So he weathered all the storm and was being oh so bold
Coming near the springtime he met his little mate
She's living in the nest and that's where she'd wait
For her little chicks were born in the early early spring
So he stood on the top branch and there he would sing
He's so proud of his family and that's where they played
They loved their little treehouse it's where they have stayed

Brotherly Love

Playing in the long grass is little Milly mouse
Who lives with her family in a tiny house
She came across a building with a door slightly ajar
Shall I go in or shan't I or will it be too far
I scurried across the wooden floor hiding by the toys
I hid inside a little shoe when I heard a lot of noise
Put your shoes on said the mother we are going to the shop
I ran so frightened in a cupboard and hid behind a mop
When it was safe and very quiet I took off to go outside
So I slipped under the door way which wasn't very wide
As I was going straight home I was crying for my mother
I ran so fast afraid to stop and bumped into my brother
Don't cry Milly I will take you home and you'll be safe with me
Mam and dad cried out thank goodness
now we are one big happy family

Ollie the Owl

Ollie the owl lives high in the rafters inside a little barn
He shares it with his mate and some sheep
who were brought here in a van
What's up said Ollie to the sheep we are all going to have a lamb
So we'd like some peace and quiet before we become a mam
Oh said Ollie to his mate a stork will be here very soon
It will be easy for the stork to find its way
as tonight is a bright full moon
The owl stayed awake all night long but the stork never came at all
Ollie cried out twit a woo hoping the stork hears his call
He was tired by the morning and fell fast asleep
and couldn't stay awake anymore
So he slept all day missing the stork who
delivered the lambs which were four
Then Ollie said to his mate oh look at the
lambs their all sleeping on the hay
Yes she said to Ollie giving him a big smile and I
know the stork will come to us one day

The Badger family

Mr. and Mrs.. Badger and their two cubs lived
deep in the heart of the woodland
The cubs were too small to be left on their own
so their father was giving a helping hand
They were named Boris and Becky as they were sister and brother
As they were growing up they were playing,
running, jumping and chasing each other
Their parents told the cubs to be aware of all the dangers
The best thing to do is run home when you see any strangers
One day they followed a trail in the woods
when they saw a little house
Don't go in there or you won't come back out said a little mouse
Then a man stepped out from the big green
door run said the mouse quick run
So the two little cubs ran so fast that they
certainly didn't call this any fun
Where are we said Becky to Boris I don't
know but we can't be far from home
I'll never do this again said Becky when we get back
I'll promise mam and dad never to roam

They walked along a path near the river's edge I remember
this place said Boris home is just over there
Mam dad they called out as they reached home sorry mam and
dad we will listen next time as we love you and really care

a Bird Meets a Bird

My name is Lady Penelope and I am a ladybird
When I say I'm doing anything I always keep my word
You can always recognise me as I'm red with black polka dots
I can also fly around and land on any greenish spots
A lot of people pick me up and tell me to fly home
But I like to go from plant to plant that's where I like to roam
Then a bird came swooping down I thought it was going to eat me
I'm sorry I frightened you said Mr. Bird
I'm looking for a worm you see
Can we be friends my name is Bertie bird
and I'm Lady Penelope a lady bird
What a coincidence our names end in bird
We may be belonging I'll tell everybody what I've heard
Goodbye lady Penelope please say you'll be my friend
The little ladybird said we will Bertie we will
always be friends right up to the very end

The Cat's Next Door

I've come to the shop to see you aunty Deny
I'm hoping to buy something for a penny
It could be a bone or a little toy
Believe me aunty Deny I have been a good boy
I've bought a toy so I'm going home
To show Toby and Lollie before they roam
They are my good friends and live next door
Oh Toby stops tormenting Lollie you're becoming a bore
We can all play together and have some fun
Till our mothers call us in when the day is done
Goodnight aunty Deny, Toby and Lollie
We've had such a good day as we've all been so jolly

My Pet Poodle

◇◇◇◇◇◇◇◇◇◇◇

Benjie my poodle is a naughty little dog
He comes with me every time I go for a jog
He barks at the people as we go through the park
He lifts his leg everywhere to make his mark
He will not come back when he is called
He looks back at me as if he's appalled
As I'm telling him Benjie don't be long
As what he's doing he believes it's not wrong
He's only a toy poodle who thinks he's so big
In the house he rules and don't care a fig
He lets himself known when he wants to be fed
He looks sweet and innocent when he's sleeping in bed
His character outshines for him to be
The best little poodle in the world to me

My Son Milo

◇◇◇◇◇◇◇◇◇◇

Milo they called him he's a big Doberman
He's nearly all black with a little bit of tan
He's loving and gentle just like a little lamb
He's such a big softie and still with his mam
They try and teach him some things to do
Lexie his mother is helping him too
Do learn these tricks we are trying to teach
If you're a good boy we'll go to the beach
So we got in the car and went for a run
All play together and we'll have some fun
We ran in the sea and fetched a few sticks
Paddling back milo learned some new tricks
On the sands we played with a little ball
Right behind us we heard a loud call
Come on everybody it's time to go now
Don't play up milo or you'll get a row
Just lay by my side and go to sleep
And on the way home we didn't hear a peep

Sam's Day Out

Sam, Sam I called out in vein
Come for a run with us again
I jumped in the car and went for a ride
Ending up stopping by the seaside
So I ran on the beach and played by the sea
Till mam and dad called me for my tea
A seagull flew down and swiped my food
That's naughty cried Sam your very rude
Never mind said mam and dad you've been such a good boy
Well take you to the shop and buy you a toy
On the way home I cuddled my ball
Thank you mam and dad I love you from Sam Mindenhall

Dilly Duckling

I am a little duckling learning to swim with my mother
I'm not the only one I have sisters and a brother
I try so hard to keep up and I know I'm very small
Come on Dilly go a bit faster or you'll end up over the fall
Over I went I felt so scared but struggled to the side
I scrambled up onto the bank and laid down just to hide
I didn't know where I was so I called out to the birds
Please help me find my mammy if you can understand my words
Of course we understand you and we will help to show the way
You follow the path along the woods whatever you do don't stray
Don't stop and talk to anyone until you reach the end
Go over the hill and down the lane then go right round the bend
There you will see your mother and family swimming on the river
I ran so fast and feeling so tired I called out with a quiver
I'm sorry mam I was so scared and am glad to be back from that fall
Mum put her wings around me, your safe
now Dilly you're back with us all

Tivy the Toy Poodle

My name is Tivy after Tiverton in Devon
My mistress says I'm the best thing next to heaven
She takes me to the park to play and have fun
To meet my friend Alfie round the field we will run
Hello you birdies whose pecking on the ground
We won't bark to frighten you or make a sound
There's squirrels over there running up and down the trees
Be careful shouted Tivy there's a nest full of bees
Thank you replied the squirrels then we went on our way
The next thing we saw were the rabbits out to play
But when they saw us they ran straight down a hole
Look over there said Alfie there's Mrs. Mole
Oh yes said Tivy will she come and play with us
No said Alfie her family comes first it's whom she'll fuss
Hello Mrs. Mole how is your family today
Very well she said but I haven't got time to stay
It's time we must go said Tivy to Alfie Moon
We'll meet here tomorrow before the afternoon

izzie the Chihuahua

Please little Izzie are you coming out to stay
Yes said little Izzie if you'll come in here to play
So we ran back and foe chasing after the ball
We hit a flower pot over which smashed against the wall
Through the window mam shouted go and play on the grass
And stop being so naughty Alfie and Izzie be a good lass
On the lawn we played until Mrs. Spider called out
My little ones are frightened when you're treading all about
You've broken my home, I've got to spin a new house
As over by the shed you've terrified Milly mouse
Up popped Mr. Beetle, what's going on it's
like an earthquake down there
We were running said the dogs we are so sorry you know we care
Anyway it's time to go in said Izzie to Alfie
My mam is taking me to Aunty Jo's café
So long little Izzie I'll see you soon
Thank your mam for having me love little Alfie Moon

Crompton the Little Saviour

Hello Crompton said Alfie can I come in if you don't mind.

I heard you are brilliant looking after Steven as he is blind.

I would like to do some good if you could tell me what to do.

Me to said Rufus the rabbit I'd like to help and that will make us two.

Alfie said Crompton you'd make the elderly very

happy as the home is down from here.

Rufus you could go to the under privileged

children but it takes longer than a year.

We will send all the other animals to get some good advice.

As you know Crompton you may be young

but you are good at being very wise.

By the way said Alfie how did you get Crompton for a name.

Richmal Crompton who wrote Just William

that's why I've got the same.

Then Crompton said we will do our very best to help the human race.

If the animals and humans will get on it will

make the world a better place.

Giving a Helping Hand

There is a story I'd like to tell and now I shall begin
I am a little Yorkshire terrier and my name is Pippin
My best mate Chicco is a Shih Tzu who is going deaf and blind
Come on Chicco come and play ball as the saying
goes you've got to be cruel to be kind
So Pippin keeps his best mate going even though he's nasty on times
Come on Chicco you can do it as he always moans and whines
Then one day our mistress took us to her best friend's house
She told us we have got to behave and be quiet like a mouse
Then she told the people that I was friendly
but Chicco is a little waspy
There was Chicco being so friendly that he was not at all so nasty
Well well said our mistress he's never done anything like that before
Well done Chicco said Pippin I hope you won't be grumpy anymore
Chicco and Pippin were very happy and enjoyed the rest of the day
We said our goodbyes and jumped in the
car and now we are on our way

My Little Friend Bella

Hello Bella I've got to say you're looking very beautiful today
I'm Alfie moon and I live across the road opposite you by the way
People think that schnauzers always look as if they are nasty
But I know you're not a bit like that not even a little bit waspy
Please don't run off down the road like that again
You could get knocked down by a car or bus or maybe a train
Bella please you must not frighten your mother like that anymore
Not all animals are lucky like we are as we have everything in galore
Come into my garden said Bella we can
chase one another and have fun
I've got a ball we can play with as we'll have
plenty of exercise when we run
After an hour passed Alfie said it is nearly time for me to go home
I've got to go soon or my mother will think
that I have gone off to roam
It's time to clean up after us and make sure we won't get a row
Your mother might let us play again if we tidy up right now
Everyone thinks a lot of you Bella and I hope
you'll be my friend to said Alfie Moon
If Marie your mother don't mind I'll come over
tomorrow sometime in the afternoon

The Loveable Miniature Schnauzers

Our names are Rosie and Poppy as we love to play all day long
Mom and dad reckon we are wicked and we
don't realise we are doing wrong
Both of us loves chasing a ball and enjoy having a good run
Things always seems to happen to us when we are having lots of fun
We knocked a flower vase over and it smashed all over the floor
It made such a noise it frightened us so we hid behind the door
A cupboard was open curiosity took over so we had a look inside
As we pulled everything out mum walking
in so we forgot to run and hide
What have you two been up to said mum making this awful mess
Come on who's the culprit said mum who's going to confess
They looked up with that innocent look as if
they had not done anything at all
She turned her head smiling I just melt when I looked
at them picking up their toys and a ball
Come on Rosie and Poppy your food is
ready and then it's time for bed
Goodnight god bless my little ones you'll
sleep well now you have been fed

Dad said butter wouldn't melt in their mouths
looking at them sleeping by there
Rosie and Poppy the lovable pair are lucky they
have a loving home and lots of love and care

alfie's friend Sandy

◇◇◇◇◇◇◇◇◇◇◇

Hello sandy it is nice to meet you walking out with your mam
I'm Alfie I live just up from you I'm alright
sandy I'm as gentle as a lamb
I heard you have two little pups in the family
and that you've become an aunt
Yes said sandy but I find it hard to keep up
with them I know I just can't
Never mind said Alfie come and play with
me we can still have lots of fun
I promise I won't be very active for you as I know you cannot run
We'll play with a ball kicking it back and forth to one another
You try sandy as Benjie can do it as he's blind
and I know because he's my brother
They were kicking the ball when it went through
the greenhouse and broke a pain of glass
Mam came out who did that she said I did said
Alfie I kicked it and sandy missed the pass
We'll clean it up said sandy and Alfie no
said mam I will clean it up now

If any of you get a nasty cut we'll have to
take you to the vet some how
Its time Alfie went home now so say goodnight to him sandy
If you're good tomorrow, you can play with sandy said
mam thanks said Alfie that would be dandy

Pidge the Pigeon

What's the matter pidge said Alfie I've lost my
speed so I can't enter for the race
Don't worry said Alfie we will find it we'll meet
here by the shed as this will be our base
I'll go and ask my brother Benjie and all my family
we can cover more ground that way
We will meet nine o'clock tomorrow and make sure
that all of us will be here by the next day
The next day we were all at the base and we
were heading to go into the woodland
Everybody chipped in to find pidges speed they
were all glad to lend a helping hand
The first one they saw was Mr. Squirrel Alfie
said please have you seen pidges speed
No said the squirrel go and see the wise old owl
he'll tell you so make sure to take heed
On the path he met Mrs. Rabbit and Mrs. Mouse please
have you seen pidges speed he's lost it somewhere
No they both said go and see the wise old owl he will tell
you as he lives down at the end of the path towards there
On the way they met Mr. Fox have you seen pidges speed asked
Alfie no he said go and ask the wise old owl he lives up in the tree

Which tree said Alfie the last one at the end of the woodland said he
When they reached the tree Alfie said please Mr. Owl can you
help us find pidges speed as he has lost it and we can't find it
Well said the wise old owl he's got to exercise
flap his wings and press ups to keep fit
With the help of Alfie and family pidge started to
exercise and he did this for a long while
Pidge entered for the big race and he said to
the others this is more my style
Oh said Benjie it's a long race I hope pidge can make it as it's very far
They all waited patiently as they could see them coming Alfie
said its pidge he's in front Hooray he's won he's a star
Alfie turned to Mr. Owl and said now I know
what it means to lose your speed
We would never find it the way we were looking
thank you Mr. Owl thank goodness we heeded
you yes said the wise old owl yes yes indeed

Becoming a frog

I am a little tadpole who's swimming in the pond
With my family and my friends whom we are very fond
We eat and swim all day long until the time is right
Then I turn into a frog and that's a beautiful sight
I'm hopping here and hopping there trying to find my way
I'm croaking off and on all day and that's what I'll say
We were all basking on the stones in the summer sun
When we were all fooling around and having a lot of fun
I croaked so loud when I hurt my leg a boy put me into a bag
Don't cry little frog I'll bandage your leg with this old bit of a rag
I'm Danny and I will be your friend so don't be frightened of me
As when your better I'll take you home so
don't worry little frog you'll see
So Danny kept his promise to take the little frog back home
I'll come and visit you very often so make sure to stay and don't roam

The Little Grass Snake

I am a little grass snake and nobody likes me at all
I slither in the grass and bushes and sleep just under a wall
I poke my head out to the sun when it's shining down on me
As I was moving in and out I heard a buzzing bee
A ball came rolling towards me as a little girl called out
Please Mr. Snake can I have my ball I'm
scared of you and I'm in doubt
No need to fear me little girl I'm only a grass snake you see
Here's your ball please be my friend and come to visit me
Why don't you live under our shed as you'll be safe under there
I'll always come to see you just hide underneath anywhere
My name is Slithers what's yours said the snake Oh I'm called Marie
I do have a friend said Slithers I know now
that not everybody hates me

Hopping Mad

My name is Gwilym the grasshopper I hop all day in the grass
My friends name is Gilly and she's a beautiful and lovely little lass
We play together most of the time and sometimes enjoy a little fuss
We click our heels playing the cricket song
and that's how you recognise us
Then one day a wasp came by and started to annoy my mate
I told him to stop he would not listen as she got into a terrible state
I was so angry I was hopping mad so I punched him in the face
I knocked him out so when he came around he flew off as if in a race
You'll be fine now Gilly as he won't bother you anymore
I hate them wasps they are always annoying
me even when I tell them to go
I will protect you and look after you if you
always stay with me you'll see
Yes said Gilly I'll always stay with you good said
Gwilym it will always be you and me

Playing Cat and Mouse

◇◇◇◇◇◇◇◇◇◇

There is a little spider spinning its web most of the day
It's to catch a fly for his supper but that's what he thought by the way
By the time he had finished he was so tired that he fell fast asleep
All the flies were flying around he didn't catch one to keep
The older flies were wiser and were playing cat and mouse
The spider said you may be teasing me I'll
catch you one day with my house
He decided to spin another web right next to the one he had spun
So to fool the flies when the sun shines on
them they will think it's only one
Then he waited quietly pretending to sleep through the next night
When a tiny fly got caught in the web he was terrified with fright
Please Mr. Spider don't eat me as I'm not very fat and I'm not very tall
As I'm not very tasty as you can see I'm only small
He took pity on the fly and told him don't come near here anymore
Thank you Mr. Spider I'll never forget you
and thanks for letting me go

Dear Oh Deer

As I was walking through the woodland I came across a deer
I knew he was hurt I tried to help as he had a look of fear
Don't worry little deer I'll look after you
as I covered him with my coat
So I carried him to my car passing my house I left a little note
I got him to the vet he looked at him saying
I'm keeping him in for a while
I phoned every day to see how he was knowing
this is not normally my style
After a week the vet told me he was ready to go back to the wood
I asked if I could be there as I'd like to see
this through knowing that I should
When I met the deer we both looked at each
other and felt this bond between us
Going up to him whispering I'll see you soon giving him a little fuss
I went to see him often and he always came running to me you see
I gave him some food telling him I love him
and his eyes said it all for me

A Right Old Rave up

Call all our dogs together Benjie said little Alfie Moon
I've decided we'll become a band and start practicing very soon
Let's all go into the shed and we can sort out what to play
Milo will play the drums Lexie on the piano Molly
and me the guitars and we'll start today
What about me said Benjie well you make the
most noise so you can be the singer
We'll all get our instruments ready come on
Benjie start to sing and don't linger
So we practiced a few hours every day for about a month or two
When we are all very good we'll go to the park and have a do
By the way what are we going to call ourselves Alfie
well he said the Moon Beams if that's Okay
That's brilliant they all said we are definitely
ready to go to the park and play
We will invite all the other animals to come and have some fun
They all said yes and couldn't wait for the day to be done
So that night they all came dancing and
twirling and doing their own thing
What a great time everybody is having said Alfie come
on Moon Beams rave it up and lets all sing

The Rose and the Bee

I am a little rose bush and I'm living on my own
In a garden full of weeds and in the centre stood a stone
I tried talking to the stone but it would not talk to me
The weeds don't like me or my thorns but I can hear a bee
Hello Miss Rosie would you mind if I have some pollen today
Have you heard the news Miss Rosie a gardener is coming here to stay
Yes you can have some pollen and no I have not heard the news
The gardener is coming in a few days and his name is Mr. Hughes
I am glad I won't be on my own I hope he's doing a rose garden
Me to said the bee then I can call my friends
and we can all have plenty of pollen
When the summer came we were all in
bloom and was taking in the sun
Then the bees came along collecting pollen from
the roses and they didn't leave a single one
You are all looking so pretty said the bee
from yellow to pink, red and white
As your garden is the best and looking so beautiful and bright
Thank you said the roses you bees can always come to us

We've got to go back to the bee hive now or
the queen will make such a fuss
Bye Bye Rosie and friends we will come and visit you soon
Bye little bees as the sun was setting they all bent
their heads from the bright full moon

it's Not impossible

I am a little red squirrel and I made friends with a little grey one
Our names are Rupert the red and Gavin the
grey and together we have lots of fun
Nobody knows of our friendship and if you do please don't tell
As our families will not like it and I know not all will be well
Then one day they all found out and that started a terrible row
Oh said Rupert to Gavin we'll try and get them
in the barn and Gavin replied how
Well said Rupert we'll tell them there's plenty of
nuts for everyone in the barn over there
So they all ran to the barn thinking they could
fill their pouches but it was all bare
Please listen said Rupert and Gavin we need to get
on with one another as this is not a game
We may be different colours but inside we are all the same
We can show all the other animals how to get
along so try and don't let us hit a brick wall
Let's not quarrel anymore and let us all be friends
as there's plenty of room for one and all

Henry the Herring

I'm Henry the herring living with my
family down in the deep blue sea
I go in and out of the reeds and rocks playing
hide 'n' seek so they can't find me
We are a big shoal who likes to have fun
especially when we go for a swim
Our scouts watch over us and let us know
when trouble is about in a whim
As the rumour say's I'm tasty when I'm cooked
and put with chips on a plate
I'm going to make sure I'm not caught at the
end of the line eating their bait
When the trawlers pass by we make sure we are
not caught and the nets don't get their fill
That when danger occurs we all hide and try to keep very still
My mother called out Henry make sure you stay by my side
As when a shark or a whale comes in sight
we've got to be quick and hide
Why is there so much danger all around us said Henry to his brother

Well I don't really know said his brother but
it's all part of nature said his mother
Keep swimming little Henry we will look after
you, so mind you keep up the good fight
So enjoy your life and stick to the rules and you will always be alright

adam the ant

I am Adam the ant living on a mountain with my very large family
There's thousands and thousands of us inside
the little hills living so very happily
We are the busiest little insects who likes working all day long
I work with my brothers and sisters and know we are very strong
Adam lookout said my brother as a human came running passed me
You're very lucky moving so quick you
could have been flattened said he
Now that was a narrow escape said Adam picking up a leaf
Quick let's take all these leaves back before we have anymore grief
On the way home they met a spider he said
I'll catch you one day in my web
Not if we can help it said Adam we'll be smarter
than him said my brother Zeb
When they got home they told everybody about their scary day
We could do without another day like today said
Adam as he laid down near the hay
Goodnight they all said feeling safe in their home at last
They couldn't keep their eyes open anymore
as they were all sleeping so fast

Jack flash

I am a young foal and I don't know what to do
My mother is a jumper and she said that's what I should do to
My father is a race horse and he reckons that's what I should be
I am torn between the two of them I love
them but I just want to be me
I tried jumping to please my mother but I was not happy at all
Then I entered a few races to please my father
but I felt I was hitting a brick wall
As I was walking around the paddock I know I was feeling very low
My friend whispered why not enter the Grand
National that should please them said Joe
Now that is a good idea as there is running and
jumping in it and that should please them both
Will you be my jockey said Jack flash our colours
are black and white and we can go forth
Then I will do my very best to win and
hope my parents will be pleased
I'll be a proper jumping Jack Flash, as they always
call me that and that is why I'm always teased
The big day came we were led towards the
start and put straight into the stall

When the flag dropped I ran so fast and jumped
so high I was afraid that we would fall
Before I realised we had gone passed the winning
post I was surprised that we had won
Now I know what I want to do as I'm ready to try
and beat the record of the famous red rum
I know my parents are very proud of me and
they realised I had to find my own way
I was driven back to my stable thinking I have solved my problem
and now I can relax to enjoy my hay (the rest of the day)

The Green Forest School

The bell was ringing for all the young animals to go to their classroom
I am Miss Gertrude your teacher I'm a Great Dane
and school is not all doom and gloom
Well animals you've got a lot to learn we won't
waste any more time so we had better begin
Your first lesson is about woodland and country
as it can be the best place to live in
I'm going to tell you about the dangers of
life and the bad that it could bring
Do not disturb any bees or wasps as they can give you a nasty sting
Some animals can eat corn, oats what the
farmers grow and also plenty of wheat
Now you've got to know which berries, leaves and nuts
are safe as they could be dangerous when you eat
You dogs and cats are lucky as you can eat from
home and also enjoy the woodland all around
While the rabbits and moles are living
burrowed deep down in the ground
We know that the hedgehog likes to live near the
gardens as that is where they get their food
There's also foxes, badgers, mice and rats some
can be cunning and some can be rude

The birds build their nests on the top branches
and squirrels live in the hollow of a tree
So animals if you learn all the rules of the woodland you
will feel safer and also live knowing you are free
Then the bell rang to tell us school is finishing for the rest of the day
Just remember what you have learnt as I will test you
tomorrow as you've got to know it all by May

Topsy and Turvey

Hello Mr. Policeman please can you help us we
are lost and don't know where to go
Our names are Topsy and Turvey we are little
penguins who are scared and feeling low
Please Mr. Policeman our mother went into the sea
to bring us food and hasn't come back at all
Come with me he said we'll go around the beach
and over the rocks in case she's had a fall
On the way, we came to a shop and Mr.
Policeman bought us some fish
Topsy and Turvey you eat this all up as it will
make you strong as it's a very good dish
Well little penguins come and show me where about you were staying
As your mother could be calling for you and
that is where she could be waiting
We can hear our mother calling said the little penguin's
quick let's go and find her said Mr. Policeman
The Policeman said they got lost so they did the right
thing to come to me by the way my name is Dan

Thank you Dan said our mother I'll never forget what you did I'm sorry we've got to go before the tide will turn Goodbye Mr. Policeman said Topsy and Turvey please come and see us next year when we return

Polly the Parrot

Polly please stop singing you're a parrot and you know you can't sing
You're supposed to copy people so listen and
don't hide your head under your wing
I know I can sing better than you said Carrie the
canary at least I can keep in tune alright
Will you stop squawking at each other said the shop
keeper it's enough to give anyone a fright
After a few days Carrie started to sing again and
all the animals joined in and loved it
You've got such a beautiful voice I could listen
to it all day said a little blue tit
Then Polly started pouting and turned her
back on them all and started to rant
Don't be like that said everybody at least
you can talk human talk we can't
She jumped on her perch spread her wings and
started to speak the human language
The shop keeper made sure that everyone was bedded
down and the parrot locked in her cage
Then Polly started to say Polly put the kettle on and we'll all go away
I hope said Carrie we can all stay together and
be good friends forever and a day

flying High

I'm Freddy the eagle living high up on a rocky mountain
Oh Dear said Freddy look at them dark
clouds I think it's going to rain
Don't worry said his partner Erin we'll cuddle up together in our nest
The chicks won't be hatched yet so we can do with a good night's rest
When the rain stopped Freddy went flying
high to focus on some food
He glided down near the woods and caught
his pray feeling in a good mood
Then he took it back to Erin and they both enjoyed their lunch
I'll tell you what said Freddy I'll go and fly high
over that mountain as I have a big hunch
Now there's loads of lamb's wool oh dear there's a
fox over there I've got to warn the sheep
I squawked so loud at the sheep so they all ran to
protect their lambs as the lambs started to weep
How can we repay you said the sheep can I
have some wool to put in our nest
There's plenty of wool over there pick out what
you need as the quality is the best
I took the wool home giving it to Erin she said
this should keep us lovely and warm

When the chicks are hatched this will keep them
safe as its better up here than the farm
After the chicks were hatched he was so proud now
we are one big happy family said the eagle
This mountain is our kingdom and this will
always be our home as it is so regal

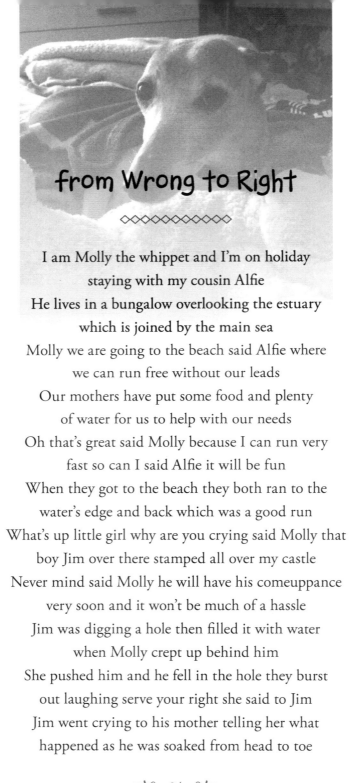

from Wrong to Right

◇◇◇◇◇◇◇◇◇◇

I am Molly the whippet and I'm on holiday
staying with my cousin Alfie
He lives in a bungalow overlooking the estuary
which is joined by the main sea
Molly we are going to the beach said Alfie where
we can run free without our leads
Our mothers have put some food and plenty
of water for us to help with our needs
Oh that's great said Molly because I can run very
fast so can I said Alfie it will be fun
When they got to the beach they both ran to the
water's edge and back which was a good run
What's up little girl why are you crying said Molly that
boy Jim over there stamped all over my castle
Never mind said Molly he will have his comeuppance
very soon and it won't be much of a hassle
Jim was digging a hole then filled it with water
when Molly crept up behind him
She pushed him and he fell in the hole they burst
out laughing serve your right she said to Jim
Jim went crying to his mother telling her what
happened as he was soaked from head to toe

That was not very nice said Alfie as he could

have had a row of his mother you know

Look said Alfie you know you should not have

done that two wrongs don't make a right

You are right said Molly the boys gone so I can't

make a mends I agree it wasn't a pretty sight

Alfie, Molly called their mothers it's time to go home as it's gone late

As they got home Molly said to Alfie I know you're

my cousin but you are also my best mate

A Swimming Lesson

Alfie Moon and all his friends decided to go for a swim
I cannot swim said a little Scotty dog who's name is Tim
Don't worry little Tim we'll teach you and show you what to do
You flick your paws back and forth I know you can do it to
All the dogs were enjoying themselves splashing about in the pool
Then little Tim got in trouble don't worry said the
Saint Bernard everybody keep their cool
I'll fetch him said the Saint Bernard when Tim came back
he said I've learnt my lesson I'm sorry I feel such a fool
Tim Alfie said the notice board is over there so make sure you stick
to the rules so enjoy yourself and stay in this shallow part of the pool
I cannot read said Tim it says 'Danger' said Alfie
don't go beyond the marker to swim
Thank you for saving my life Mr. Saint Bernard
I will listen to you all said little Tim
They all had great fun swimming back and
forth and inviting everybody around
Then it was time they all made tracks for they
made sure they were all homeward bound

Printed in Great Britain
by Amazon

19752205R00057